First World War
and Army of Occupation
War Diary
France, Belgium and Germany

41 DIVISION
Divisional Troops
238 Machine Gun Company
18 February 1917 - 30 September 1917

WO95/2627/5

The Naval & Military Press Ltd
www.nmarchive.com
Published in association with The National Archives

Published by

The Naval & Military Press Ltd

Unit 10 Ridgewood Industrial Park,

Uckfield, East Sussex,

TN22 5QE England

Tel: +44 (0) 1825 749494

www.naval-military-press.com

www.nmarchive.com

This diary has been reprinted in facsimile from the original. Any imperfections are inevitably reproduced and the quality may fall short of modern type and cartographic standards.

© **Crown Copyright**
Images reproduced by permission of The National Archives, London, England, 2015.

Contents

Document type	Place/Title	Date From	Date To
Heading	WO95/2627/6		
Heading	41st Division 238 Machine Gun Coy 1917 Jly-1917 Sep To Mesopotamia 18 Ind Div. 54 Bde		
War Diary	Belton Park	18/02/1917	18/02/1917
War Diary	Grantham	18/02/1917	13/07/1917
War Diary	Southampton	13/07/1917	13/07/1917
War Diary	Le Havre	14/07/1917	16/07/1917
War Diary	Abeele	17/07/1917	17/07/1917
War Diary	Meteren	17/07/1917	18/07/1917
War Diary	Piebrouck	19/07/1917	23/07/1917
War Diary	Westoutre	23/07/1917	31/07/1917
War Diary	Bivouacs		
War Diary	Westoutre	01/08/1917	05/08/1917
War Diary	In The Line	06/08/1917	14/08/1917
War Diary	Elzenwalle	14/08/1917	14/08/1917
War Diary	Pierbrouck	15/08/1917	20/08/1917
War Diary	P Of W Camp	21/08/1917	21/08/1917
War Diary	Wizernes	22/08/1917	08/09/1917
War Diary	Dickebush	09/09/1917	25/09/1917
War Diary	Caestre	26/09/1917	28/09/1917
War Diary	Ghyvelde	29/09/1917	30/09/1917
Miscellaneous	'A' D.H.Q.	01/10/1917	01/10/1917

W005 / t292 / 樹9

41ST DIVISION

238 MACHINE GUN COY

~~FEB 1917 - DEC 1918~~

1917 JLY — 1917 SEP.

To MESOPOTAMIA
16 IND DIV. 54 BDE

Army Form C. 2118.

WAR DIARY
or
INTELLIGENCE SUMMARY

(Erase heading not required.)

238 Machine Gun Company
Machine Gun Corps

MGC I

Place	Date	Hour	Summary of Events and Information	Remarks and references to Appendices
Belton Park	18/2/17		Formation of Company	
Grantham	2/7		Equipping and training ten days of workshop personnel	
Grantham	13/3/17	3.30am	Departed from Grantham	
Southampton	do	12.15pm	Arrived	
do	do	6pm	Embarked	
Le Havre	14/3/17	3am	Disembarked and marched	
do	do	2.30pm	Arrived at Rest Camp, Sanvic	
do	15/3/17		Moving from advance to complete Entrainment provided no Prevent, Abbeville and Hazebrouck.	
do	16/3/17	2pm	Unsuccessful Detrained. Attached to Hd Quarters as Divisional Machine Gun Coy.	
Abeele	17/3/17	4pm	Arrived in Billets	
Meteren	to 18/3/17		Settled Billets	
do	do	9am	Arrived in new Billets	
Pre Brouck	do 19/3/17	10am	Arrived in new Billets	
do	20/3/17		Training	
do	21 "		Inspected by Major General S.T.B. Lawford C.B. Divisional Commander. Training.	

Army Form C. 2118.

WAR DIARY
or
INTELLIGENCE SUMMARY.
(Erase heading not required.)

Sheet II

Place	Date	Hour	Summary of Events and Information	Remarks and references to Appendices
PIEBROUCK	July 1917 22	3.30am	2 Officers 26 Other ranks (No 3 Section) marched to KRUISSTRAATHOEK to act guides to relieve on relief of 194th S.Cy. in the new positions of the HOUIEBEKE sector. 34 men from No 144 M.G. Coy attached for accommodation rations.	
do.	23		Vacated billets & marched to WESTOUTRE.	
WESTOUTRE	23	4.30pm	Bivouacked in BROOKECAMP. Pt M.16.a.5.8. (Belgian Trench Sheet 28 Part 3.)	
do.	24.-		Camp work.	
do.	28.			
do.	25.		No 3 Section returned to billets from trenches.	
do.	29.		3 Officers & 155 + 24 men + 16 mules attached to No 141 M.G.Coy to practise pack mule	
			to the at RENINGHELST.	
do.	30.		Pack mule party now upt. proceed area. Remainder of section work	
			in Camp.	
do.	31st		Section work in Camp.	

[signature] Capt.
O.C. 239 M.G.Cy.

Army Form C. 2118.

WAR DIARY
or
INTELLIGENCE SUMMARY

(Erase heading not required.)

238 Machine Gun Company

Ship 1. Vol 2

Place	Date	Hour	Summary of Events and Information	Remarks and references to Appendices
Busseboom	Aug 1917			
Westoutre	1&2.		No training parade	
do	3.		O.C., section Officers & Sgts proceeded up to the line to reconnoitre.	
do	4.		Preparing Gun Kit etc for the line.	
do	5.		Company relieved 194 M.G. Coy in Brigade position in the HOLLEBEKE Sector. All 16 guns in line. Transport & stables remained in WESTOUTRE.	
			1 N.C.O. & 1 O.R. slightly wounded by shrapnel wound.	
Jutka line	6–14.		In the line	
ELZENWALLE	14.		Company relieved by 205 M.G.Coy. Marched back to shelter the Long Hut at ELZENWALLE.	
PERROQUET	15.		Transport and stables treated camp & marched to PERROQUET Khujan. Company bivouaced at HALLEBAST CORNER and avenue to Company. Men Rink at 7.50pm.	
do	16		Cleaning all Gun Kit etc	
do	17		Inspection by D.M.G.O. at 9pm	
do	18–19.		Training at Hut	

Army Form C. 2118.

WAR DIARY
or
INTELLIGENCE SUMMARY.
(Erase heading not required.)

238 Machine Gun Coy

Sheet 2

Place	Date	Hour	Summary of Events and Information	Remarks and references to Appendices
Quernes R.	Aug 19		Church Parade. Fernandez & Gray putting up open to move	
do	20		Attached to 123 Bde for march etc. Left billet at 6am marched to Quernes 8	
			Was Cay per Rayonchr.	
Pops Camp	21		Marched 9½ at 10.30 arrived in bivok at WIZERNES at 4 p.m.	
WIZERNES	22		Cleaning up all equipment.	
do	23		Training. Lecture by Cay S.O. (C.R. Biller)	
do	24		Inspection by the C in C. at Le Fosse Farm at 11 am Division having	
do	25		O.C. acting for Bde fo whilst the brother is on leave.	
to	31		Training except in billets owing to inclement weather.	

J.D. Welchimp
Capt
OC 238 M.G. Coy

Army Form C. 2118.

WAR DIARY
or
INTELLIGENCE SUMMARY.
(Erase heading not required.)

238 Machine Gun Company

Sheet 1. 4/1/3

Place	Date	Hour	Summary of Events and Information	Remarks and references to Appendices
WIZERNES	1-8.		September	
	3.		Training as per programme laid down by Div. Attachments of 38 M. pins to S.B. provides & Abeele to Art. coveng defence.	
do.	8.		Remainder of Company proceed to DICKEBUSH. lection from 194 M.G. Coy and taken over M.G. attached to work on the line preparatory to relieving.	
DICKEBUSH	9-15.		Work on line, preparing trenches etc. for many purposes. Covered so 4 to take positions.	
do.	16.		The detachment from ABEELE informed the Company.	
do.	17.		Two sections went into the line to complete work. 48 of 4th attached to Coveng.	
do.	18.		Remaining two sections went into line.	
do.	20.		Attack day. All 2 + 5 guns delivered programme barrage fire.	
do.	22.		Has to relieve to Reigned Rouse.	
do.	23-24.		Remained in lines disposing S.O.S. calls + doing harassing fire.	
do.	25.		Relieve by 229 M.G. Coy. Returned to Camp in DICKEBUSH. Total Casualties 15 Killed. 3 died of wounds 39 wounded.	

Army Form C. 2118.

WAR DIARY
or
INTELLIGENCE SUMMARY.
(Erase heading not required.)

238 M.S. Coy

September

Place	Date	Hour	Summary of Events and Information	Remarks and references to Appendices
DICKEBUSH	25.		Entrained at DICKEBUSH. Detrained at CAESTRE.	
CAESTRE	26+27.		Reorganising + cleaning up. Transport proceeded by road to WORMHOUDT. Dept of 30 O.R. taken from Base.	
do.	28.		Entrained for GHYVELDE. Arrived in camp at Nursery. Transport arrived at 4 p.m.	
GHYVELDE	29		To be ready to proceed overseas on 24 hrs notice. Received orders from Division	
do.	30		Drafts from 144 & 149 M.S.Coy both giving ? improved personal & complete establishment. Much to prepare to carry out ordinary etc.	

J.A. Welsh? Capt.

G.81/338

A
D.H.Q

Herewith original War Diary for
September please

[signature]
for OC 235 M.G. Coy

1/11/17

www.ingramcontent.com/pod-product-compliance
Lightning Source LLC
Chambersburg PA
CBHW081617160426
43191CB00011B/2166